Reconciliation
for
Spiritual Growth

Experiencing the Sacrament Anew

By Rev. Bill Murphy

Pauline
BOOKS & MEDIA
Boston

Nihil Obstat: Rev. John J. Connelly, S.T.D.

Imprimatur: †Bernard Cardinal Law
Archbishop of Boston
April 11, 2000

ISBN 0-8198-6472-2

cover photo credit: Sr. M. Emmanuel Alves, FSP

Printed and published in the U.S.A. by Pauline Books &
Media, 50 Saint Pauls Avenue, Boston MA 02130-3491.

www.pauline.org

Pauline Books & Media is the publishing house of the
Daughters of St. Paul, an international congregation of
women religious serving the Church with the communica-
tions media.

1 2 3 4 5 6 7   05 04 03 02 01 00

"Come to me, all you who are weary and find life burdensome, and I will refresh you"

(Mt 11:28)

If you have picked up this pamphlet you already have a sense that the path to deep peace in life winds through a spiritual landscape. Circumstances have probably shown you that placing supreme importance on money, status, or possessions guarantees only disappointment. Relying on particular individuals to bring us happiness places upon them expectations that they cannot possibly fulfill, no matter how wonderful they may be. Looking around, we find that the truly peaceful people in our midst are those who place their trust in God. Reliance on God is the way to go.

Being Human

Despite this truth, it becomes clear to any sincere believer in God that the life-journey along a spiritual path can be burdensome. Belief does not assure us of a trouble-free existence. Hardly. Believers and their loved ones fall ill and die. We have trouble at work and in relationships. We repeat patterns that cause trouble for us and for those in our lives. A life of faith can be difficult.

Some of our troubles cannot be predicted, prevented, or avoided. Much of what goes on in life is far beyond our control. However, experience teaches us that much of the difficulty we have in life is due in part to our own behavior. The disruption of our relationships, a sense of distance from God, and a feeling of discomfort with our own selves can often be traced to attitudes and actions that arise from within us. For various reasons, we feel compelled to go against what God has revealed to us about right living. When you and I consciously choose to act in a way we know is against what God has taught, we call that sin. Life lived in sin grows increasingly difficult. Gradually, we experience a deepening emptiness inside. We become isolated from a positive experience of human companionship. We become less sure of our place in the world. Most distressing of all, we wonder where God went.

Our faith assures us that God desires our company. God created men and women so that we might know the joy of living life in communion with the Blessed Trinity: Father, Son, and Holy Spirit. However, this relationship is not forced on us. God gave us the capacity to choose this gift in order that we might fully appreciate it. Naturally, one would think that only a fool would choose anything but life with God. But we all fall short. Every person knows the momentary thrill of choosing an action just to please him or herself. We all know what it's like to think we've found real and lasting happiness through material gain or emotional contentment. It feels like we've discovered a shortcut. It feels like a stroke of independence and maturity. In truth, it is a movement against our nature. Again, reliance on God is the only way to go.

God desires that we grow familiar with life's spiritual option. God seeks to nudge us back into a life lived in accord with spiritual principles and truths. When sin has wearied us and laid a burden on our hearts, God desires to relieve us and restore us. In a real and magnificent way, God has already restored us through the willing sacrifice of Jesus Christ on the cross. In that great act, God did for us what no other person could ever have done: God forgave the sins of all humanity. All human sinfulness was reconciled to God, forever assuring us that God will not hold our actions against us if we seek to live in Divine communion.

The problem of alienation from God arises from within us. Just as each man and woman remains free, so each individual comes to know the reality of sin personally. However, when we do, God desires that we come to an awareness of our sin, turn boldly away from it, amend any damage we have caused, and live refreshed in the grace freely given. The communion between Earth and Heaven, which was completed through the life, death, and resurrection of Jesus Christ, once again becomes our most vital source of inspiration. We are set free.

This gift of God is the gift of restored and deepened unity. It is available to us in the Catholic Church through the sacrament of Reconciliation. The purpose of this pamphlet is to help you to revisit this sacrament. Perhaps it has been some time since you made use of this offer from God. Perhaps you feel a little stale in your practice of confession. It may be you'd like to go a little deeper than you're used to. The reason doesn't matter. It is always good to prepare anew. Your efforts will bring you greater self-clarity. Greater clarity will bring you closer to God's liberating truth.

What the Sacrament of Reconciliation Can and Cannot Do

Expectations largely determine our perceptions of life. We may feel that life has little meaning unless we are being satisfied. If we believe that the world should cater to our needs, we will frequently be dissatisfied. On the other hand, if we secretly expect to find no comfortable place in the world, we won't. If we feel that people won't like us, we will silently communicate that message and will end up not attracting friends. When you and I approach the sacrament of Reconciliation, we need to be clear about its purpose and best use. If we expect the sacrament to give us a feeling of purity, light, and holiness each time we make use of it, we will probably be disappointed. Most people do not have that felt experience, even when conscious of the wonderful things God does for them through the sacrament. On the opposite end of the possibility spectrum, there are those who expect nothing useful from the sacrament. They feel it is hypocrisy to seek forgiveness for sins that they may well commit again. They feel that confessing to another person is unnecessary. These persons, if they make use of the sacrament at all, may point to their unchanged heart and say, "See, I told you nothing would happen." Most likely, persons who feel this way don't even go to confession.

So, what are reasonable expectations of the sacrament of Reconciliation? Let's consider three.

First: God is present.

In this sacrament, God the Father, through the power of the Holy Spirit, makes present and effective once more the unconditional love displayed by the life, death, and resurrection of Jesus Christ. Receiving the grace of this sacrament is a spiritual event. Although we are participating in it, it may not make us feel different. We do not have a reliable and consistent perception of grace in the same way that we can recognize stimuli of the physical world (light, heat and cold, sound, etc.). Our emotions may not shift right at the moment of sacramental forgiveness, but in faith, we are assured the event of forgiveness has happened.

God desires that we grow in the divine image and likeness in which each human person has been uniquely created. God promised from the beginning of creation that divine assistance would always be available. Jesus Christ told those gathered around him when he was about to ascend into Heaven, "I am with you always, to the close of the age" (Mt 28:20). The coming of the Holy Spirit is God's presence until the end of time. There is never a moment of life when you or I are without God's company.

God never dismisses any person as unimportant. We are all precious in God's eyes. We all hold a position in God's heart as unique and unrepeatable expressions of his love. No matter what kind of mistakes we make, no matter how selfishly we may act, no matter how much wreckage we leave in our path, the situation is never hopeless because God is always present, eager to help if we ask.

Second: We can expect the sacrament of Reconciliation to be *work*.

Driving an automobile through an intersection when the traffic light is green takes minimal effort, especially to an experienced driver. That kind of activity is not personal. We do not have to invest much time or effort in it. Like so many daily actions, it seems almost automatic. Seeking forgiveness through the sacrament of Reconciliation can become like that. It can become routine, uneventful, and unsatisfying. Once a person has learned a workable form of the ritual, as many of us did at age seven or eight, only a mild case of the butterflies distinguishes going to confession from going to the bank. As was mentioned earlier, this experience of "routine" may be what has prompted you to look for a more fulfilling one.

The practice of the sacrament of Reconciliation is meant to be a regular practice, but not a routine one. Looking to be reconciled to God and to those in our lives is a highly personal affair. It requires our time and our focused attention. We make a search of our thoughts and behavior. We recall those actions of which we are not proud. (How easy it can be to let them slip our minds!) We sift through those recollections for clues to our motivations. We then hold those motivations up for judgment against our consciences and the teaching of the Church. We need to be willing to accept ourselves and to make specific plans to change our ways. This thorough approach to reconciliation is work indeed. The good news is that once it is engaged, it becomes easier over time, and more effective, too.

Third: We cannot expect everything to happen at once.

Patience with ourselves is essential. Reconciliation to God and other persons can take place at potentially every level of our being, but especially where we have any formed opinions about life. And we need to keep this in mind particularly when we try to uncover deeper motivations. For example: if I am in the habit of stealing office supplies from my workplace, I can confess this each time I steal and hope that God's grace changes me into a more honest person, which it may. Or, I may seek God's strength when I am faced with the stocked shelves of the supply room and a rising desire for pens or sticky notepaper. In either case, I am trying to address the problem with God's help, but I am only going at the *symptoms* when there may be an underlying *cause*.

With the sins I repeat and cannot seem to be rid of, chances are there is some deeper, unseen motivation. Otherwise, why would I keep doing it? This deeper reality, like a hidden root of a plant, will continue to show itself through new growth unless I work to find and remove it. To apply this to our "office thief" example: Perhaps I am used to being treated poorly. Feelings of inferiority may be so much a part of me that I don't see them. I am trying to distract myself from their effects by taking something new without paying. The thrill will mask my poor self-image. By stealing index cards or erasers, I am somehow trying to "fix" myself. I mistakenly believe that I might apply a material solution to an emotional problem. To thoroughly address this sinful behavior, then, I need to understand my motivation.

Being open to this kind of revelation comes only after much experience. That's the way we learn. God rarely heals a sinner completely and for all time. That is because God ordinarily heals only what we are able to bring to him. Remember, our freedom plays a big part. It takes a long time to want to uncover deeper motivations, and still longer to get at them. We need to be patient.

Enlisting a Companion

One certain way of deepening the experience of Reconciliation is to meet regularly with someone who will come to understand you. A trusted companion will hold a memory of your weaknesses, growth, and goals. We are often too close to our own lives to be objective. We may not notice repeating patterns in our lives, but they may be obvious to someone else. If you seek consistency and long-term spiritual growth, it is wise to keep a regular schedule of confession with the same confessor. It may also be helpful to meet from time to time with a spiritual director. If your spiritual director is a priest, these roles may overlap. In fact, it is easier if they do. When your spiritual director is a priest, you will not have to be concerned with forgetting (or omitting) something significant when you move from one meeting to the next, or from reflection to a celebration of the sacrament. Your spiritual director does not have to be a priest, however. Many superb spiritual directors are religious men and women and dedicated lay persons.

The roles of confessor and spiritual director are not identical. It will help to try to understand how each plays a part in the experience of reconciliation. Spiritual direction occurs when a person enlists another's help in exploring the personal realm where relating to God occurs. In the history of the Church, this guiding accompaniment has taken many forms. Even today, there is no official approach to spiritual direction. Various methods come in and out of popular use. In some cases, the spiritual director consciously shapes the directee according to a specific way of relating to God. Here the relationship centers on instruction and formation. In other cases, the director listens carefully to the directee's explanation of recent prayer experiences, thoughts, and behavior and helps the directee to identify God's call. Here the director observes and points the directee back to his or her experience through his or her own words. In some relationships, the meetings are loosely scheduled and the conversation seems to flow into different areas each time. Some people find this helpful, especially if they are just beginning to acquaint themselves with a structured spiritual life.

Perhaps what binds together all forms of spiritual direction is that they occur with some regularity between the same persons, and that the goal is a deeper communion with God. It is a relationship committed to the time and effort needed to allow a person to unpack that interior space where beliefs are formed. It is an open-ended process by which a person strives to know him or herself clearly, and to deepen an authentic response to God. No person is ever finished with spiritual direction. There is no "graduation." There may come a time when the directee wishes to discontinue meeting for a length of time, or change directors, but as long as we have life within us, the stage is set for further growth in God. That means there is always something to discover.

Much of the work involved in improving one's experience of the sacrament of Reconciliation may take place in spiritual direction. Here, the heart is opened, a person takes honest stock of him or herself, and time is spent in prayerful reflection on the nature of the beliefs held in one's deepest heart.

The practice of the sacrament is designed to make use of what has been learned about oneself. In a sense, spiritual direction uncovers and examines the very depths that will benefit from the grace of the sacrament. Sometimes in confession a priest will try to address the deeper issues brought forward by a penitent, but the amount of time ordinarily available does not allow for much of that. If you invited a food critic over to your house to evaluate your cooking, you wouldn't present your guest with a bag of unprepared groceries. In the same way, the confessional is not a practical place to begin and end the process of self-discovery. In order to respect the complexities of your own interior life it is important to have worked at knowing yourself prior to meeting with your confessor.

Not everyone has the opportunity to spend significant periods of time with a spiritual director or in prayerful reflection. Here is where it is especially helpful to choose one priest as your confessor and stick with him. A priest who hears your confession on a regular basis will be able to provide some of the depth, continuity, and insight that we expect of spiritual direction. He will come to know you. He will be able to challenge you to look hard at issues that keep returning. He will be able to remind you of progress you have made and spiritual consolations you have received. He will be your link to your past and point you toward a fuller communion with the Lord. He will be able to do this with a spirit of pastoral concern and Christian fellowship.

Just a note on the kind of relationship you might expect from your confessor or spiritual director. Like a physician, these individuals come to know you very well. In time, you may become friends with these supportive persons. However, their primary role and responsibility is to provide you with a service, not to befriend you. Do not be disappointed if this is not your most significant relationship. It is not meant to be. It is meant to assist you in imitating Jesus Christ as you go about living in the relationships that are most significant.

Examination of Conscience

Another valuable tool available to us as we seek to know and deepen our spiritual lives is the examination of conscience. This is work we do alone, apart from and prior to meeting with a spiritual director. It is "preparation for preparation." When we do not have the opportunity for regular spiritual direction, a careful examination of conscience provides the framework for uncovering instances of sin, destructive patterns, and hidden motivation.

"Conscience" is that intangible dimension of our person which knows most clearly the will of God. The concept of conscience is beautifully described in the *Pastoral Constitution on the Church in the Modern World* (Gaudium et Spes) of the Second Vatican Council.

"Deep within...man discovers a law which he has not laid upon himself but which he must obey. Its voice, ever calling him to love and to do what is good and avoid evil, sounds in his heart at the right moment.... For man has in his heart a law inscribed by God.... His conscience is man's most secret core and his sanctuary. There he is alone with God whose voice echoes in his depths" (n. 16).

Conscience *advises* when action is planned, and conscience *judges* when action is taken. This mysterious dimension of the human person is given to us by God to be developed into a source of reliable guidance as we set about making free choices. When it comes time to form a clear vision of our spiritual progress, it is the conscience that holds the truth.

Many persons find it helpful to "question" the conscience by way of a structured reflection. This is called an "examination of conscience." Formulated, objective questions allow one to proceed thoroughly through one's recent history. When preparing for the sacrament of Reconciliation, an examination of conscience is invaluable.

There are as many ways to examine one's conscience as there are approaches to the spiritual life. For the Christian, an examination of recent behavior ought to somehow center on the living example of Jesus Christ. Christ, the second person of the Trinity, lived with an unparalleled divine authority. His life perfectly reflected God as expressed in the life of a human person. We call ourselves disciples of Christ, and so we need to judge our own actions according to the words of Christ or by some organized reflection on his earthly presence.

For example, the Ten Commandments are a popular tool for evaluating personal behavior. Although they predate the arrival of Jesus, there is no disagreement between Jesus Christ and the Ten Commandments. In fact, Christ came to fulfill the Law given to Moses. The Ten Commandments offer a thorough guide. The words of Christ himself as found in the Beatitudes of Matthew's Gospel (cf. 5:3–12), offer a more reflective method. They present the virtues necessary for relating to God, relating to other persons and living the faith as a public person. You may also want to consider Saint Paul's summary of what it means to live apart from Christ, and what it looks like to live in harmony with him. For this, look to Paul's Letter to the Galatians, chapter 5, verses 16 to 25. These standards have come to be known as the "works of the flesh" and "the works of the Spirit." They offer a precise and direct measure of behavior. Paul, a spiritual writer of great richness, also proves a helpful guide in his description of Christian love found in 1 Corinthians 13:4–7. Another method to examine conscience uses the centuries-old formulation of the "seven deadly sins." A careful reflection regarding the sins of pride, anger, lust, envy, gluttony, avarice, and sloth usually provides a realistic picture of where healing is needed.

How you put resources such as these to use is up to you. Some persons take an account of their lives each evening or at some other time during the day. This creates a sharp interior awareness. Others wait until they are preparing for a meeting with a spiritual director or a celebration of the sacrament. Like any good tool, an examination of conscience is only helpful when it is used. Make this practice a part of your life and you will find tremendous benefit from the growing self-awareness.

All Spiritual Growth Is Reconciliation

Oftentimes we associate Reconciliation with Advent or Lent. Parish priests usually experience their greatest demand for the sacrament of Reconciliation in the days before Christmas and Easter. Communal penance services are organized, preachers emphasize the need for conversion, and people gather to receive forgiveness.

There is obvious value in giving a penitential theme to a specific time of year, but the work of reconciliation ought not to be limited to certain days or weeks. *All* spiritual growth is reconciling, no matter when it takes place. That being so, reconciliation becomes something attractive at all times and in all situations. To see how, let's take a step back and look at the big picture.

When God created our first parents, Adam and Eve, their lives were as perfect as could be imagined. They lived in innocence. They lacked nothing. They moved with God freely, heard God's voice, and benefited from God's abundant creativity. In order that they might be truly free creatures, God established a prohibition on one of the trees in the Garden. They were not to eat of the fruit from the Tree of the

Knowledge of good and evil. Adam and Eve abused that freedom. They crossed the boundary God had set. We are the children of Adam and Eve. We are like them. We share in that same tendency toward doing what we want, even if we have been told otherwise. We are always on the lookout for chances to bend reality to the shape of our desires.

This tendency is present within us when we are born. It is part of our nature to test and disregard the boundaries God asks us to freely observe. As we grow from infancy into youth, we do much more testing and disregarding than obeying. Often, our parents or other adults keep us in line through fear of punishment. They are, after all, so much bigger—and they buy the food! During these early years, we form images of God. God is like our parents, except that God sees all, is everywhere, and has the power to reward or punish far beyond our parents' ability. Even in the best of situations, this model for understanding God is limited. The example of even the most wonderful parents cannot properly express who God is. Our parents cannot be adequately compared to God. We are bound to misunderstand. Persons who grow up in difficult or even abusive situations will have an even harder time understanding God as all powerful and all loving. For those who have been damaged by adults, it is easy to question or reject the concept of a loving God.

Because of our tendency to be rebellious and self-centered, and by our early experience, we are more than likely to misunderstand God. God as revealed to us as Father, Son, and Holy Spirit is not something that humans naturally comprehend. Coming to a deep and true understanding of God takes considerable thought, much prayer, and the willingness to make adjustments according to all the shifts and changes of life experience.

Can you see how every movement toward greater understanding is an act of reconciliation? Each time we integrate the experience of our lives with the teaching of the Church, we grow. We step toward God. We become more like Christ: enlightened, aware, and humble before God's great majesty. Gradually our childhood images of God give way. They have to. They ought to.

Some of the stages along the way toward a fuller understanding of God should be familiar. For instance, we have to accept the fact that God will answer our prayers, but according to the divine will, not ours. We have to deal with the repeated reality of suffering. We are challenged by the omnipotence of God in the face of the evil sometimes chosen by human beings. We have to make adjustments to our sense of God each time we learn new things about ourselves or accept new responsibilities. The reality of God takes on new dimensions for us when we leave the familiar environment of our childhood home for the first time. It changes when we set about to support ourselves with shelter and food. It shifts and takes new shape when we grow close to other persons, and especially when we begin to develop exclusive, committed relationships.

How the image of God changes when new life is brought into the world! Then, the mantle of responsibility shifts to one's own generation, and the unspeakable joy and rebellious autonomy of one's own children are experienced firsthand. God begins to look very different when one's parents grow sick and die, and when the aging process becomes more obvious in the mirror, when there is no longer another generation standing between us and eternal life. Finally, adjustments must once more be made when one senses the approach of death. At each turn, God becomes a different reality for us. Of course, it is not God who has changed; we have. As we see and experience more of life, we are challenged to integrate our faith with the different shapes of living.

Reconciliation: A Way of Life

The reassuring truth is that God is there to meet us when we arrive at each place of newness. What frightens us most about change is the deep-seated fear that in this new place we will not be safe. We are concerned that we will not have God to rely on in the same way we've known. Perhaps we even know the panic of believing that this latest transition will reveal God's absence. That panic is often enough to prevent some people from moving into a new understanding of God and the spiritual life. The terror of being alone puts a stop to a forward movement and the old understanding of God is retained, even if it no longer functions well or fails in answering significant questions. Like a toddler who hangs on to its crib blanket until the thing is smaller than a folded handkerchief and as filthy as a curbstone, we can try to hold on to what worked in the past, even when we know it won't work now.

So, in a very real sense, the most significant tool we are given for life is that of Reconciliation: Reconciliation to life as it is, Reconciliation to God as God is, Reconciliation to ourselves as gifted but flawed individuals, and Reconciliation to those who have been hurt by our selfish actions or unkind words. Life is a long series of opportunities for reconciliation—accepted or refused. Each time we are willing to step forward into greater truth, we are courageously trusting that God will be present in the new situation to bring us into harmony with a new understanding of life.

Jesus Christ so often encouraged his disciples, "Do not be afraid." He did so because his relationship with the Father was so complete that he knew the power and goodness of the Father's love would overcome the terror and panic of uncertainty. The life of Jesus Christ was one of constantly stepping forward into life with little else than the deep belief in the power of truth as protection and defense. As a result, his life was marked by countless moments of reconciliation. He stepped across social lines, spoke to those who were cast off, brought healing in ways that challenged rigid conformity, and never once withdrew his commitment to calling persons out of their own darkness.

For a time, Jesus seemed to have been defeated by those forces that would stop the human spirit from moving forward to the Father. Immediately following his death, it seemed as if the power of fear had won. It seemed that the yawning chasm of nothingness had consumed him. But it was not to last. On the third day, Jesus rose. Defeating the unknowable terror of death, Jesus showed to all humanity that the path to complete communion with the Father was open. Now there is nothing to prevent each of us from repeating that victorious journey to God. Easter is ours.

Courage for the Journey

The movement toward deeper self-understanding always sets in motion a more profound and authentic relationship with God. Our greatest asset in this growth is the virtue of courage. Courage is trust and a forward movement in the presence of fear. To ask for courage is not to ask that fear be removed. Fear is a natural part of our lives. To ask for courage is to ask for the strength to take the next step toward truth *despite* fear. It is to ask for faith that God's protection is near. It is to ask for hope that what lies ahead is freedom as beautiful as Easter. It is to ask for a heart that burns with a longing for eternal communion with the One who made us, a communion that will not be denied.

This reflection may seem to be removed from the commonly accessible practice of the sacrament of Reconciliation. In fact, it is meant to return us to it. The deep reaches of communion with the divine are entered through this seemingly ordinary and underused method. The work we do in preparing ourselves opens and softens our hearts. The skilled companionship of a trusted believer turns us toward different horizons where God may be more readily identified. The regular practice of the sacrament builds on itself so that when we are not in harmony with God, self, and others, we know what to do. Through what may sometimes seem a routine and mundane action, we are able to bring our deepest hearts into the presence of God, who will never forget us or stop offering us a love of inexpressible measure.

Wherever you may be in your journey to God, may you persevere. May your use of the sacrament of Reconciliation confirm God's presence in your life, free you from your fears of the unknown, and inspire you to seek reconciliation in all things. Christ *is* reconciliation. May his brotherhood embrace you, now and forever.

About the Author

A native of Boston, Massachusetts, Rev. Bill Murphy graduated from Emerson College in Boston and then entered Saint John's Seminary in Brighton. He was ordained for service to the Archdiocese of Boston in 1988. Fr. Murphy has served in two parish assignments and has also worked in the area of clergy personnel. He is currently serving as a spiritual director at Saint John's Seminary.

Pauline
BOOKS & MEDIA

The Daughters of St. Paul operate book and media centers a
the following addresses. Visit, call or write the one neares
you today, or find us on the World Wide Web, www.pauline.org

CALIFORNIA
3908 Sepulveda Blvd., Culver City, CA
   90230; 310-397-8676
5945 Balboa Ave., San Diego, CA
   92111; 858-565-9181
46 Geary Street, San Francisco, CA
   94108; 415-781-5180

FLORIDA
145 S.W. 107th Ave., Miami, FL
   33174; 305-559-6715

HAWAII
1143 Bishop Street, Honolulu, HI
   96813; 808-521-2731
Neighbor Islands call: 800-259-8463

ILLINOIS
172 North Michigan Ave., Chicago, IL
   60601; 312-346-4228

LOUISIANA
4403 Veterans Memorial Blvd.,
   Metairie, LA 70006; 504-887-7631

MASSACHUSETTS
Rte. 1, 885 Providence Hwy.,
   Dedham, MA 02026; 781-326-5385

MISSOURI
9804 Watson Rd., St. Louis, MO
   63126; 314-965-3512

NEW JERSEY
561 U.S. Route 1, Wick Plaza,
   Edison, NJ 08817; 732-572-1200

NEW YORK
150 East 52nd Street, New York, NY
   10022; 212-754-1110
78 Fort Place, Staten Island, NY
   10301; 718-447-5071

OHIO
2105 Ontario Street (at Prospect
   Ave.), Cleveland, OH 44115;
   216-621-9427

PENNSYLVANIA
9171-A Roosevelt Blvd., Philadelphia
   PA 19114; 215-676-9494

SOUTH CAROLINA
243 King Street, Charleston, SC
   29401; 843-577-0175

TENNESSEE
4811 Poplar Ave., Memphis, TN
   38117; 901-761-2987

TEXAS
114 Main Plaza, San Antonio, TX
   78205; 210-224-8101

VIRGINIA
1025 King Street, Alexandria, VA
   22314; 703-549-3806

CANADA
3022 Dufferin Street, Toronto, Ontario
   Canada M6B 3T5; 416-781-9131
1155 Yonge Street, Toronto, Ontario,
   Canada M4T 1W2; 416-934-3440

¡También somos su fuente para libros, videos y música en español